PRIMARY

Arts and Crafts

Ana Oviedo Melgares

ANAYA

Editorial coordination: Stephanie Gay.

Editor: Danny Latimer.

Adaptation: Danny Latimer and Michelle Martínez.

Design: Miguel Ángel Pacheco and Javier Serrano.

Infographic Design: Patricia Gómez and Verónica de la Sierra.

Illustrations: Carlos Díaz, Juan García González and Jesús Alonso.

Layout: Grafimarque S.L.

Correction: José Mª. Marcelino.

Graphic editing: Elena Achón.

Photographs: Anaya Archive (Boé, O.; Candel, C.; Cosano, P.; Enríquez, S.; García-Pelayo, Á.; Enríquez, S.; Leiva, Á.; Lucas, J.; Martin, Jh.; Martín J. A. ; Ortega, Á.; Ramón Ortega, P.-Fototeca de España; Ruiz, J. B.; Sanguinetti, J. A.-Fototeca de España; Torres, O.; Valls, R.) Age, Album, Efe, Getty, Thinkstock/Getty Images, 123RF (y colaboradores).

Our publications carefully select the content, illustrations and language to comply with non-discrimination due to gender, culture or opinion.
IMPORTANT: The activities proposed in this book should be completed in a separate notebook or on sheets of paper, not in the book itself.

BL000545/1E4I - 3100305

Materials

lead pencil

coloured pencils

thin felt-tip pens

thick felt-tip pens

soft wax crayons

hard wax crayons

tempera paints

glue

recycled material

scrap paper

scissors

modelling clay

Term 1

Term 2

IDEAS Project

- A Carnival booth

Term 3

IDEAS Project

- Egyptian exhibition

Term 1

The human face

Portraits and photography

The Countess of Vilches by Federico de Madrazo (1853)

Manuel Altolaguirre, The poet from Málaga by José Moreno Villa

Before there were cameras, the only way to have a portrait done was to have it painted. Royalty and important figures used to have their portraits done by painters. Many of these portraits have become famous.

Portrait of the Álvarez Quintero brothers

King Alfonso XIII and Queen Victoria Eugenia

Today, some painters and artists still do portraits, using different techniques.

Since the invention of photography, many professionals have created wonderful works of art using their cameras.

Portraits and grids

Grids can be used to help make a copy of a portrait. The copy can be the same size, larger or smaller.

La Gioconda by Leonardo da Vinci (1503 - 1506)

Copy of *La Gioconda*

- Look at the painting *La Gioconda* (The Mona Lisa) and the copy that was made of it. The copy was made using a grid.
- Make your own copy. Copy the grid on a piece of cardboard as indicated. First, draw the grid on a piece of paper with a ruler. Then, add the letters and numbers.

The use of colour

Colours and their meanings

Warm colours, such as red, yellow and orange, can be associated with the Sun or fire. They give a sensation of happiness, strength and energy.

Cool colours, such as blue, green and violet, can be associated with plants, the sea, the sky and water. These colours give a sensation of peace, relaxation and sometimes sadness.

Chromotherapy (colour therapy) is used in alternative medicine by some therapists. The idea is that different colours have different effects on our mind and body.

A poisonous toadstool

A poisonous frog

Colours can reveal a message. Nature often reveals messages to us using colour. If we see red in nature it can warn us of danger, such as when we see a poisonous red toadstool. Bright yellow and black colours can also warn us that an animal is poisonous.

Drawing with colour variation

Look at the four versions of the drawing of a figure against a background. The figure is a cat that is sitting on a ledge by the window. The picture also shows the curtains and the background colour outside the window.

The shape and colour of the cat don't change; they stay the same. The shapes of the curtains and window don't change, but their colour does. Look at the colour of the glass in each of the pictures.

- What moment of the day do you think each represents?
- In which picture do you think it is raining outside?
- In which picture is it sunny outside?
- Make two different copies of the picture and change the background colour in each.

Cartoons

Film script

A **film script** is a document that includes the dialogue, details and directions needed to make a film.

A person who prepares a script is called a **screenwriter**. Screenwriters have got to describe people, places and actions in great detail when writing a film script.

An optical illusion based on an animated film.

If a film script is written for a cartoon or animated movie there is usually more action than dialogue included in the script. Today, many cartoons and animated films are made in 3D.

How to make a storyboard

Look at the panels in the cartoon storyboard. In order to draw the panels, the screenwriter had to write the story. He/She had to write what would happen in each panel. Then, an illustrator drew a picture for each panel.

- Create your own story and a six-panel storyboard to go with it. First, write the script and then draw an illustration for each panel. Then, show it to a partner and explain what is happening in your comic.

Autumn

Autumn in art

Autumn begins on the 23rd of September and ends on the 20th of December. It is the season in which we collect the harvest (the plants that we grow for food).

A path in valle del Loira, France

An autumn landscape in Cazorla, Jaén

Autumn by Giuseppi Arcimboldo

Autumn garden by Vincent van Gogh

During autumn, the leaves of deciduous trees change colour. Green leaves turn yellow, orange or brown and fall to the ground. During this season, temperatures start to drop and the wind gets stronger and colder.

Autumn inspires artists to create works of art. It has inspired them to take photographs as well as write poetry, stories and novels.

Steps to create a fruit portrait

Giuseppe Arcimboldo (1527 – 1593) was an Italian painter. He was well known for painting the human face using flowers, fruits, plants, animals and other objects.

Look at the painting *Autumn* on page 14. Follow the steps to create a fruit portrait using Arcimboldo's style or a style similar to it.

Draw the shapes of the fruit, leaves and other objects as you draw the shape of the face and shoulders

Finish drawing the elements and add details with felt-tip pens.

Steps to create an autumn landscape with torn paper

Look at how to create an autumn landscape. You will need yellow, orange, red and brown paper, or any other autumn colours you would like to include.

Tear the paper into small pieces. Place them on a piece of cardboard to create an autumn landscape.

Tear up pieces of blue paper to use for the sky. Add fine details with felt-tip pens or wax crayons.

Photography

Photography - then and now

The first photographs date back to 1839, with the invention of **Daguerreotype**. It's a process that creates a photograph on a metal plate.

For many years, photographs could only be taken in black and white. Eventually, colour photographs were produced.

Daguerreotype. Río de Janeiro (Brazil)

A black and white photo of a bridge in Alcántara (Toledo)

A picture of Gran Vía taken in Madrid in the 1970s

A woman taking a picture with a digital camera

Today, we continue using cameras to produce photographs and digital photos. Digital photos are stored on a memory card. We can look at them instantly without the need to process and developed them in a photo lab.

What would you look like in the 19th century?

Follow the steps to create a portrait showing what you would look like if you had lived in the 19th century.

First, find and make copies of old pictures of your family and a recent picture of yourself. You will also need pictures of people who lived in the 19th century from newspapers and magazines.

1

On a piece of white or light-coloured paper, create a border using a pencil and ruler.

2

Cut out the 19th century clothing from the newspaper, magazine or copy of a family photo. Glue it onto the piece of paper.

3

Find the recent picture of you and cut out your neck and face. Glue it onto the paper so that it looks like you are wearing the 19th century clothing.

4

Colour or shade the background of your picture.

5

Decorate the border of your picture however you would like.

6

Now you know what you would look like in the 19th century!

Jan van Eyk

Portrait of the Arnolfini Couple

Jan van Eyk (1390 - 1441) was a well known painter from Northern Europe. He painted in a style known as `Primitive Flemish´. *The Portrait of the Arnolfini Couple* is one of his most well known works of art. It is of a rich merchant and his wife. In the background, on the wall, we can see a round mirror with reflections of the couple in it.

The red tones of the tapestry contrast with the elegant green dress the woman is wearing. The light in the painting can be seen in the faces and the white lace that the woman is wearing on her head. The couple is holding hands, which represents their union. The woman is resting her other hand on her stomach because she's pregnant.

Portrait of the Arnolfini couple (1434)

Margaret van Eyk (1439)

Margaret van Eyk

This **portrait** is of the painter´s wife. She was 33 years old when it was painted. She is wearing a headdress and has got her hair in two buns, in the form of horns, just like the woman in the portrait of the Arnolfini couple.

van Eyk's self portrait

Look at the examples. Choose a piece of cardboard. You can use whichever colour you would like. Find a photograph of yourself that was taken recently. Cut out your face and glue it to the upper part of the cardboard.

1a

1b

2a

2b

- If you're a boy, draw a big black hat and a cloak. If you're a girl, draw yourself in a green dress. Draw your hair with two buns in the shape of horns, with a lace veil covering your head.
- Colour your drawing with tempera paints or felt-tip pens. Decorate the background however you would like.

Human rights

Unicef

In 1948, the United Nations declared that **human rights** are fundamental conditions that all people are entitled to. They declared everyone has the right to live a decent life and should be guaranteed basic necessities. These necessities include food, clothing and a safe place to live.

Basic rights include not discriminating against people because of skin colour, the language they speak, religion, political views, or whether they are a boy or a girl (their gender).

November 20th is Universal Children's Day

The 20th of November is Universal Children's Day. This is the day that Unicef signed the document declaring what rights children had. This document is the first international document that recognises girls and boys as people with their own rights and as part of society.

The United Nations Children's Fund (Unicef) has humanitarian programmes in developing countries to help boys and girls.

Make a Universal Children's Day poster

Read the ten fundamental rights children have. Choose one of them and make a poster using newspaper and magazine cut-outs.

Use coloured text to write down the right you have chosen. Add drawings and details to make your poster attractive.

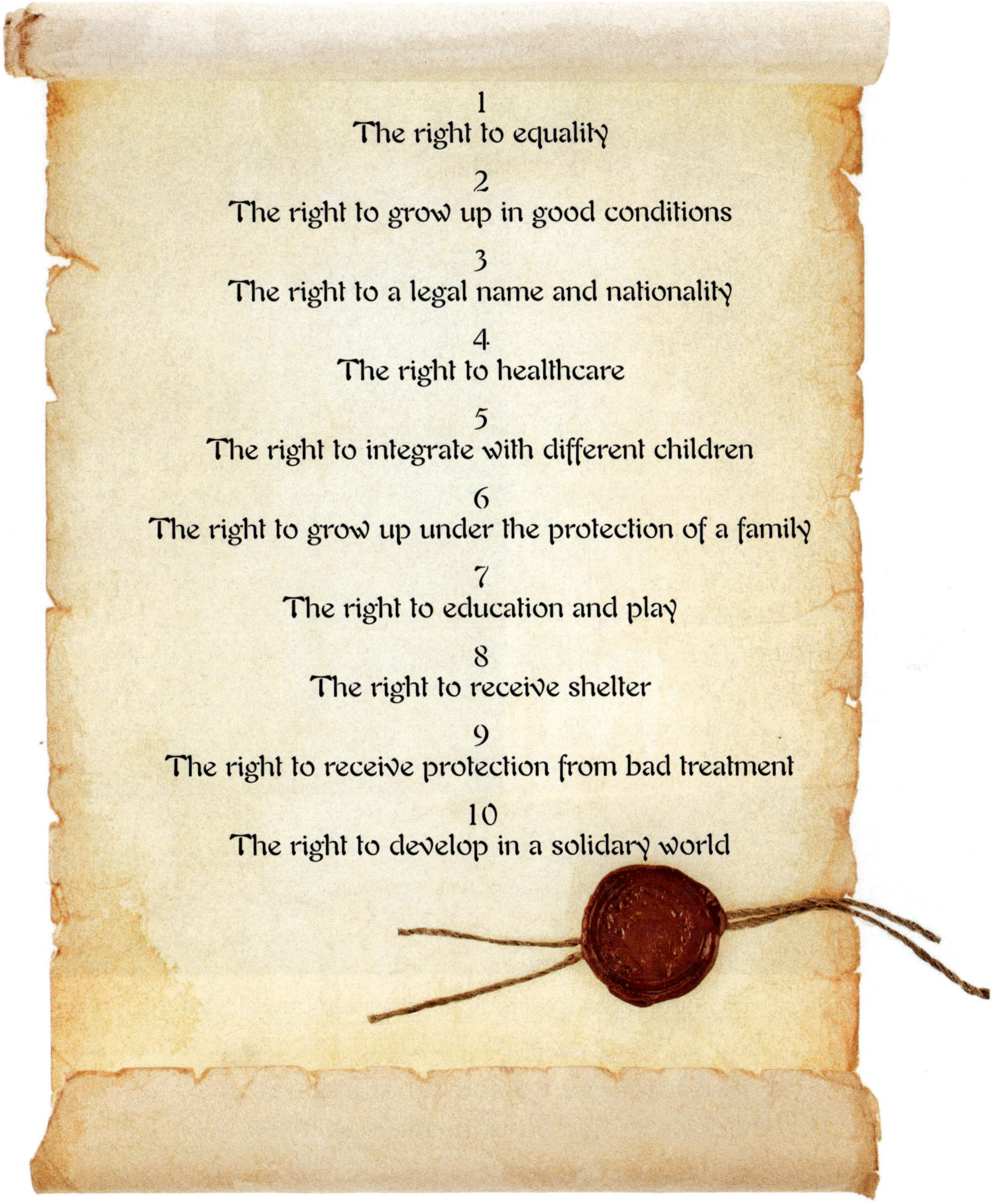

Shadows

Shadow theatre

Shadow play came before shadow theatre. It began as a popular game that used optical effects.

Shadow play is when we use our hands or other objects and put them between light and a clear surface, such as a screen or wall.

In shadow theatre, silhouettes are projected onto a screen or wall.

Shadow theatre is one of the oldest forms of theatre that involves puppets or marionettes. The shadows projected onto the screen or wall are called **silhouettes**.

A silhouette is an image or outline of a person or object that consists of one colour (usually black).

Shadow theatre

Work in a small group. Think about a scene that you all would like to act out in your shadow theatre. Which characters and objects are you going to need?

Work together to write the plot of the story; think of the characters and objects needed, and rehearse the scene.

Follow these four steps to create a shadow theatre play.

1

Cut out the shapes of people, animals or objects from magazines.

2

Place the cut-outs on a piece of cardboard and trace the outline of the shape.

3

Paint the outlines black using tempera paint. Wait for the paint to dry and cut out the silhouettes.

4

Glue a piece of string to the back of the silhouettes. Move the figures behind a piece of opaque paper and act out your shadow theatre!

Traffic signs

Geometric shapes

Traffic signs are signs that are used on public streets. They tell us (both as drivers and pedestrians) to follow certain rules. They also give us information.

Knowing what these signs mean is an important part of street safety. They tell us what rules to follow so we can get along with others. They help us avoid car accidents and to be better pedestrians.

zebra crossing

direction of taxi rank

direction of parking reserved for the disabled

no entry

turn left

no stopping on the left

wild animals ahead

school crossing ahead

slippery road

There are several international traffic signs and symbols created to help us. Words are not always necessary to convey a message. Sometimes, symbols are just as effective on their own.

These signs and symbols were made using geometric shapes.

Road safety

Road safety is very important. It includes the rules to follow both as a pedestrian and as a driver. It lets pedestrians know how to behave on streets and pavements. It lets drivers know how to behave on the road.

We should all be aware of the rules of road safety and how important it is. It helps drivers and pedestrians coexist safely.

We need to know what traffic and pedestrian signs mean. They tell us what road safety rules we should follow.

Road safety billboard

Look at the example of a road safety billboard and describe the elements that you can see.

- What do the white lines coming from the wheels and behind the car mean?
- What do the eyes and white arrow looking towards the car mean?
- What do the traffic signs you can see mean?

Create your own road safety billboard! Don't forget to include traffic signs. Include a motivational saying at the top of the billboard. For example, 'Stop, look and listen!'

Decorative art

Everyday art

Decorative art can be functional and useful. It is often made of materials such as wood, glass, metal, cloth or paper. Decorative art is different to fine art such as paintings, drawings, photography and sculpture.

Paper lanterns and colourful awnings are examples of everyday art.

Many everyday objects can be very original and decorative. Some are made of different recycled materials.

In Andalucía, there are pieces that are very typical of the region, such as garlands or paper lanterns. These can be found at parties and fairs.

Steps to make a decorative pencil case

Cut two milk cartons in half as in the picture so that both are the same shape and size.

Glue them together so that they look like a house. Decorate them with coloured paper and felt-tip pens.

Make a cardboard base for your fair stand. Decorate it however you would like.

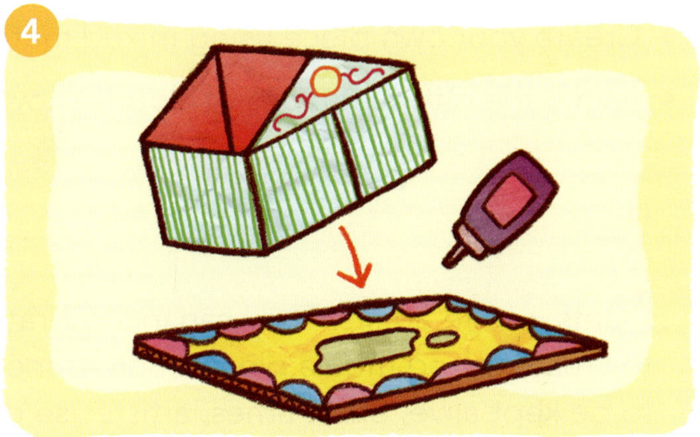

Glue the fair stand to the base.

Add decorations to your fair stand, such as paper lanterns, garlands or an awning.

Enjoy using your new pencil case!

Ideasexpress

Clouds in art

When we use two or more different artistic techniques to create a work of art, it is called a **mixed technique**. We can use mixed technique to represent different scenes from everyday life and nature. Different artists have been inspired by clouds. They use different materials to create their works.

1

2

3

- Create your own piece using mixed materials. It can be 2D or 3D.
- Name the different types of clouds shown in pictures1-3.

Plants in art

Plants inspire artists. They can incorporate them into their art to create mixed media pieces. Sometimes, the plants need to be kept alive, other times, artists use plant parts in the piece.

- How does interaction work in plants?

Eco Art

Some artists use recycled materials and trash to call attention to the fact we need to take better care of our neighbourhood and mother nature.

- We share the earth with all different kinds of animals. It is important to take care of our surroundings and protect the environment. How are ecosystems related to the environment and what different kinds are there?
- Create a poster or 3D sculpture to draw attention to our need to recycle and reuse materials more.

Steps to create an abstract composition using a mixed technique.

Paint patches of colour using tempera paints and wait for them to dry.

Add details with felt-tip pens.

Add more detail and shading using wax crayons.

Steps to create a hedgehog using a mixed technique.

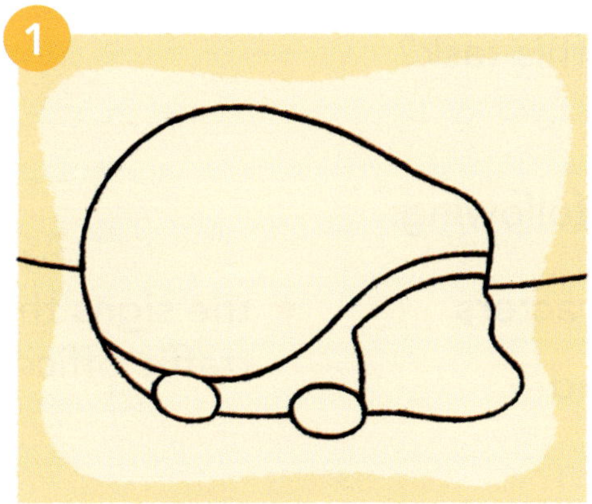

Draw the outline of a hedgehog on a piece of light-coloured cardboard.

Paint the hedgehog using tempera paints and wait for the paint to dry.

Add details with felt-tip pens.

Finish the hedgehog by adding more detail and shading using wax crayons.

IDEAS Brillant Plays

INVESTIGATE

1 Have you ever been to the theatre? What did the set look like? What did the costumes look like?

DISCOVER

The theatre company Brilliant Plays has heard that you're a great artist! They want your help designing a scene for a play they're writing. It is a comedy. It is a chaotic scene that takes place in autumn. There is lots of traffic because a silly traffic officer has mixed up his traffic signs.

2 Think about the following and write about it in your notebook.

1 What colours are typically found in autumn? This will help when designing the background. Think about the trees, bushes, clouds, costumes and lighting.

2 What types of traffic signs are there? What shapes are they?

3 How might a storyboard help you complete this task?

EXPLORE

3 Get into groups and create sketches of the following:

- a storyboard
- the background
- the cars and characters
- the characters and costumes
- the signs the traffic officer has

APPLY

4 Follow the instructions.

1 Find a cardboard box and cut out one of the sides so that you can see into it.

2 Paint the background of the set that you sketched inside the box.

3 Create cardboard cut-outs of the characters, the signs for the traffic officer and the cars. Paint them and decorate them however you would like.

SUMMARY

5 Using your storyboard for the scene as a guide, put on a play for the rest of your class using the scene and the cut-outs that you have made.

Term 2

What is craftwork?

Craftwork from Andalucía

Craftwork is work that is done by hand, without machines. **Artisans** are people who create these unique pieces of art.

Oil cruet from Úbeda, Jaén

Traditional blankets and rugs from Níjar, Almeria

Earthenware canteens from Úbeda, Jaén

Fans in a shop in Córdoba

Andalucía is a community that is rich in these types of crafts. Artisans from Andalucía use materials such as: earthenware, leather, fabric, stone, metals, wood, vegetables and fibres. You can find craftwork both in contemporary culture and in traditional trades from this area.

Symmetrical objects

An object is **symmetrical** when both halves are identical. In order to draw a symmetrical object, you must first draw an **axis of symmetry**. This is a straight line that will help you to make sure that both halves are the same.

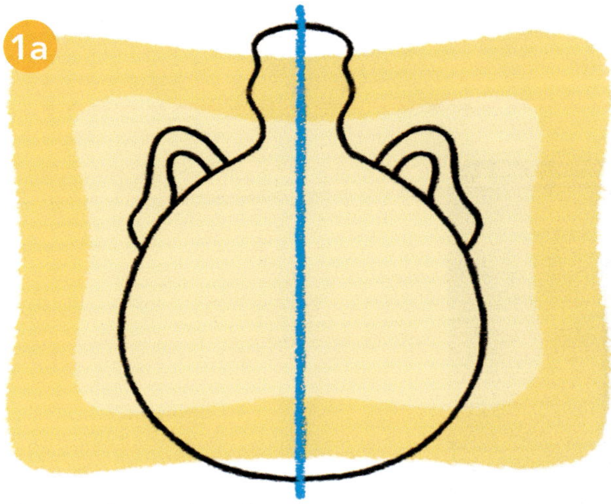

Draw the axis of symmetry on a piece of paper and then draw both sides of the canteen.

Colour your drawing with wax crayons or coloured pencils.

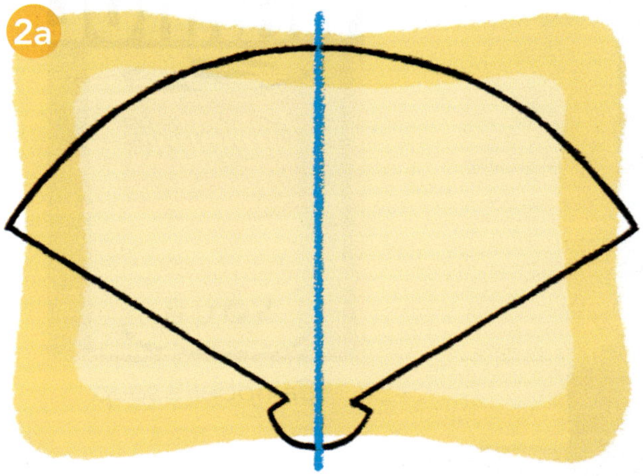

Draw the axis of symmetry on a piece of paper and then draw both sides of the fan.

Colour your drawing with wax crayons or coloured pencils. Use both light and dark shades.

How to draw and colour a canteen and a fan step by step.

- Draw the axis of symmetry and the image, position a ruler horizontally on the centre line so that it forms a cross shape.
- Make sure the measurements on either side are the same. Move the ruler to different horizontal positions to check the measurements of other areas of your drawing.
- Once you've checked all the measurements, erase the axis of symmetry so that you can colour your drawing.

Pop Art

Who is Andy Warhol?

Pop Art is an art movement from the 20th century. It's characterised by its use of everyday images from advertisements, comic books and movie posters. This movement started as a rebellion. It was different from anything done before.

Self-portrait

Campbell's soup

Andy Warhol (1928-1987) is one of the most famous pop artists. He created decorative art using canned goods, bottled refreshments and coloured photographs of famous people.

Colourful works of art

Look at this self-portrait by Andy Warhol. It was very original because of the six repeated portraits paired together in primary and secondary colours.

Create your own drawing of six repeated objects using a variation of colours. You can use Andy Warhol's portrait or these flowerpots as inspiration!

Volume

Shading with light and dark colours

Volume is the three-dimensional size of an object or a space. The dimensions are the **length**, **height** and **width**.

In art, volume can be real, like in architecture or sculptures, or it can be simulated using different techniques, like in drawings or paintings.

If we want to add volume in a drawing or painting, we have got to use light and dark colours to create shading.

Light from above, casting shadows below the chair.

Light from above, casting shadows below the flower pot.

Light from the right, casting shadows to the left of the pot.

Marbles

Draw different marbles using a compass. Colour the areas using light and dark shades like in the examples below. Create a template like the one shown.

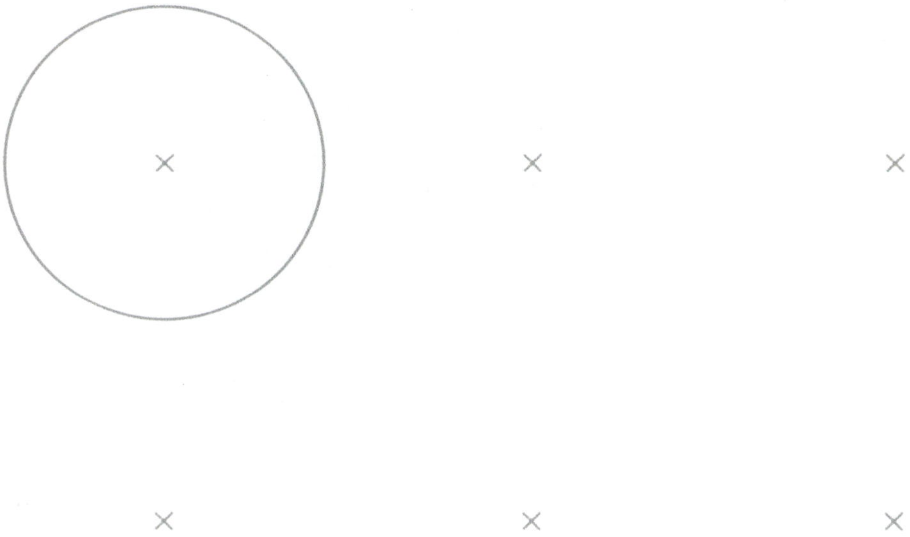

Meanings in pictures

Symbols

A **symbol** is the representation of an idea. Symbols and ideas are directly related so that many people know what they mean. A heart is a symbol for love. A white dove is a symbol for peace. Colours can also symbolise feelings. For example, green is a colour for hope.

The Sun symbolises light.

The recycling symbol.

A heart symbolises love.

A scale symbolises justice.

A dove symbolises peace.

The symbol for medicine.

- Copy the words below into your notebook and match the colours to the feeling they symbolise for you. Talk to a partner and explain your choices.

1 blue	**2** red	**3** yellow	**4** white
a) purity	**b)** happiness	**c)** love	**d)** energy, light

Peace Day Logo

A **logo** is a symbol made up of letters, pictures or drawings that represent an idea. They are often used in advertisements so that a lot of people recognise them. Can you think of any logos?

- Ever since 1964, the 30th of January has been the School Day of Non-violence and Peace. Look at the example. Work with a partner to create your own logo and poster.

Gothic style

Cathedrals, churches and palaces

The **gothic** style was developed in Europe towards the end of the Middle Ages. Gothic style cathedrals have pointed arches. They are very tall, wide, buildings with stained-glass windows to let natural sunlight in.

Priory church in Aracena, Huelva

Jabalcinto Palace in Baeza, Jaén

Cathedral with the Giralda Tower in Sevilla

Saint Paul's Church in Úbeda, Jaén

The Santa Maria de la Sede cathedral is the biggest gothic style cathedral in the world. It was declared a Unesco World Heritage Site, along with the Alcázar and Archivo de Indias, in Sevilla, in 1987. In 2010, it was named a site of Outstanding Universal Value. There are also other gothic style buildings, like churches and palaces, throughout Europe.

- Are there any gothic buildings where you live? Which ones?

How to draw a palace scene

Look at the picture and imagine what it must have been like to live in a palace in the Middle Ages. Talk about it with a partner.

An inner courtyard at a palace

1

2

Work with your partner to draw a palace scene. Think about what the people in your picture might be saying to each other. Write a short dialogue with your partner and act it out together.

Marine art

Seascapes

Marine art is a drawing, painting or sculpture related to the ocean.

Marine art can include boats, fish, aquatic mammals, the beach, corals, underwater vegetation, or anything else related to the ocean. Sometimes it even includes lakes and rivers!

Helm of a ferry in Doñana, Huelva

Guadalquiver River in Sevilla

Motril beach in Granada

Doñana beach in Huelva

We have got several provinces in our community that are on the coast: Huelva, Cádiz, Málaga, Granada and Almería. Let's not forget the Guadalquivir River that makes Sevilla one of Spain's favorite cities.

Our coastal cities are a wonderful inspiration for marine art!

- Where is your favorite place by the sea?

Draw La Caleta beach

La Caleta beach is a well-known beach in Cádiz. It's well-known for its spa built in the 1920s. Look at the pictures below to help you draw and colour the beach and part of the spa.

Draw the images and use a ruler to help you with the spa.

Use coloured pencils to colour the light tones first and then colour the dark tones.

Make marine art!

Joaquin Sorolla (1863-1923) is well known for his marine paintings like the one below. Find a piece of blue or green coloured paper and use wax crayons or tempera paints to represent the ocean. Be sure to alternate colours and use long strokes.

Sea in Javea (1905)

'Impossible' patterns

Maurits Cornelis (M.C.) Escher

M.C. Escher (1898 - 1972) was a Dutch artist known for his "impossible" patterns and imaginary worlds. He was especially interested in maths and geometry. Escher made two trips to the Alhambra in Granada where he was inspired by the Arab mosaics and their repetitive shapes.

Mosaic tiles from the Alhambra

Smaller and smaller by M.C. Escher

- Look at Escher's drawing and observe how the lizards form a design and become smaller and smaller in size.

Make your own Escher-like drawing!

To make a drawing using the same style as Escher, you need to repeat the same shape lots of times. For this project you are going to make fish all the same size, not smaller and smaller. Follow the steps below.

1

Use some cardboard and a ruler to draw a rectangle and then cut it out.

2

To make your template, draw a small triangle on one end, cut it out and tape it to the other end of the rectangle.

3

Use your template to copy and trace the shapes as shown in the picture.

4

Colour your fish by alternating the colours. Make sure the details on each fish are identical.

Drawing to scale

Plans

A **plan** is a graphic representation of a space. We make plans for lots of things, such as buildings, houses, parks and streets.

In order to draw a plan, you need to know the size and shape of the space and everything in it. We use maths to make a scale so that the plan represents the correct proportions and distances of something, but in a smaller size. A scale of 1:100 means that 1 cm on the drawing is really equal to 100 cm in its full size (which is 1 metre).

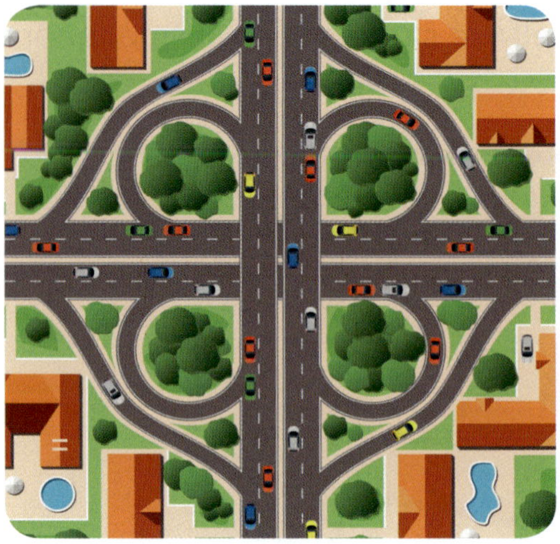
Plan of an urban area

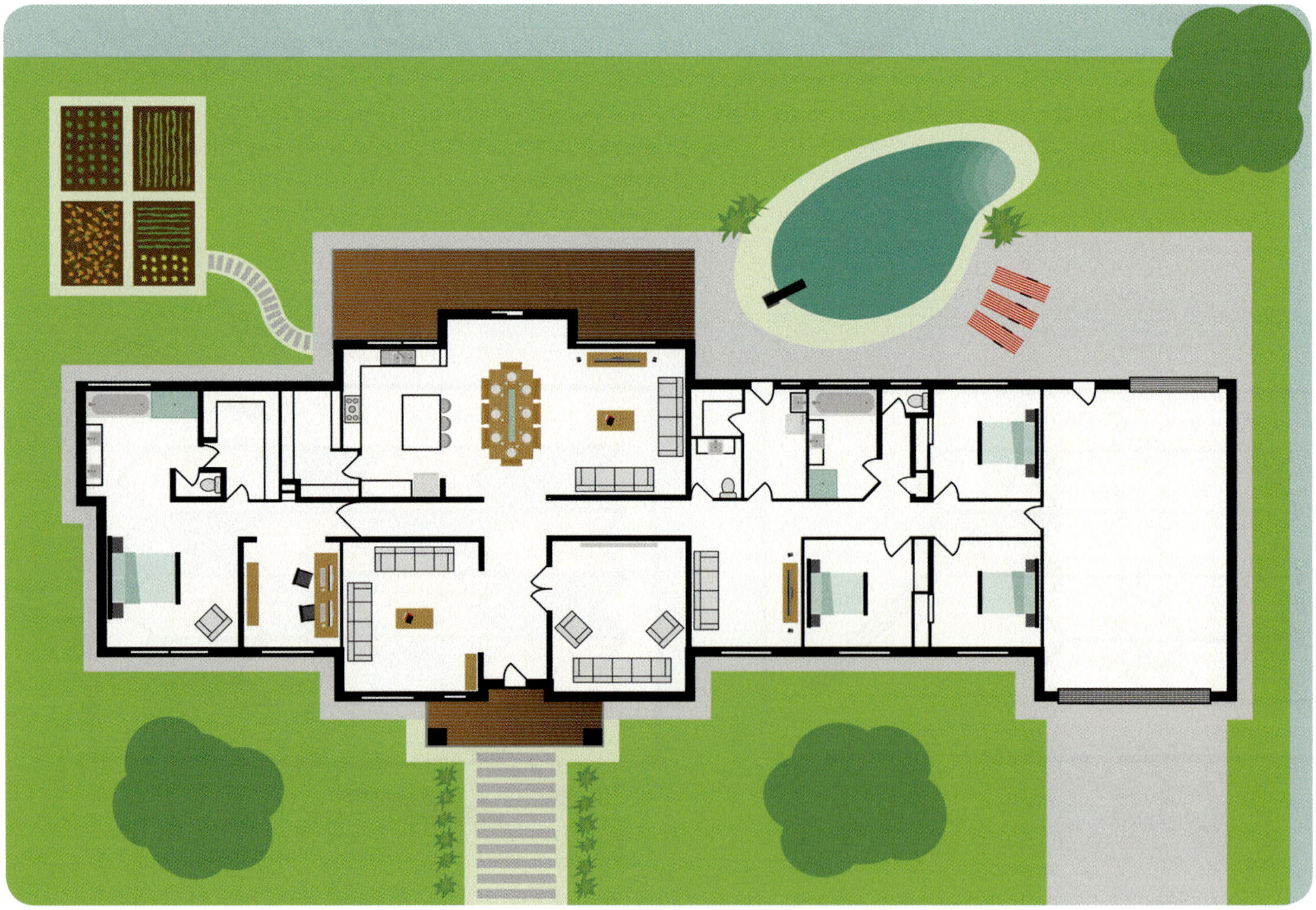
Plan of a house

Design your future flat!

The plan of a flat is useful to have so that you can see the size of each space and the way it is distributed. Look at the colourful plan below. It shows you simple drawings of furniture so that you can imagine how things will fit in each space.

Think about the flat you would like to have when you are older. Use a ruler to draw each room, its proportions and the furniture you will put in it. Use coloured pencils to make it as colourful as possible.

Textures

Collage

A **collage** is a technique where different materials and shapes are assembled to create a whole.

Pablo Picasso and Georges Braque were the first artists to make collages. Natural materials are great to make collages with because they add texture.

Texture can be seen and felt. When we touch a surface, we can feel its texture. Some textures include smooth, rough and granulate. When we look at a surface, it is easy to imagine what its texture feels like.

- What is your favourite texture and why?

Granulated surface

Cobblestones on the street

Wooden surface

Rough surface

Stone wall

Tree bark

Make your own collage!

- Make your own collage with natural materials like rice, beans, pasta, lentils and nuts. Make sure they are uncooked! You can also use sand and shells.
- Be as creative as you can when you draw your monster!
- Follow the step by step instructions below.

1

Collect the materials that you are going to use for your collage.

2

Draw a silly face or the face of a monster or alien.

3

Decorate the face however you would like.

4

Decorate the background however you would like.

Ideas express

Science in art

It's Carnival time in Greenbow. The town hall asked residents to help them celebrate.

Sharon is 67 years old. She used to be a science teacher, but no longer works. She enjoys hiking in her free time. She combined her love of art with her love of science to create pieces combining the forest and body parts.

- Look at Sharon's piece inspired by the circulatory system. Create a piece based off of another body system.

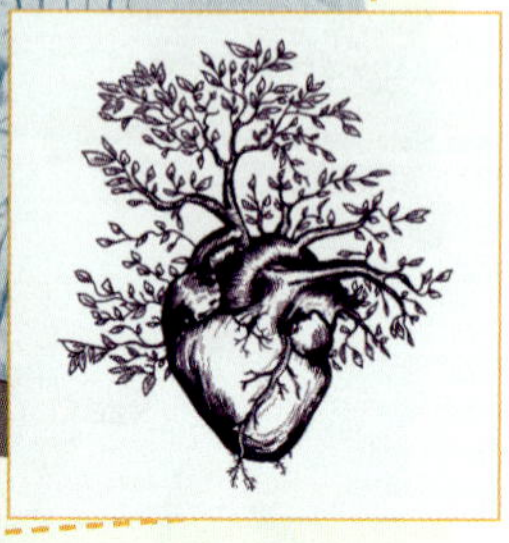

Fun food

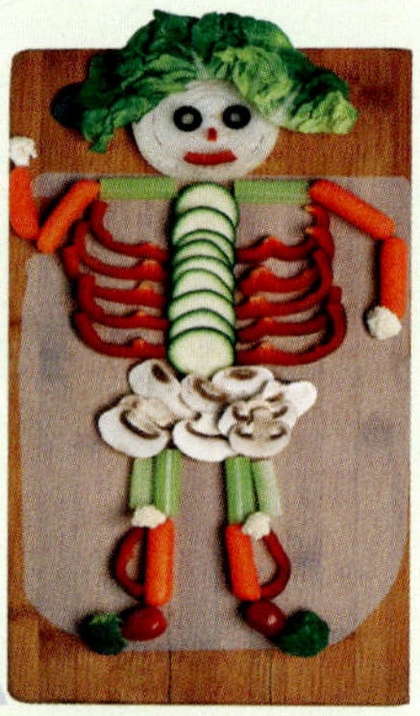

Jack works as a chef. He knows that healthy nutrition is very important. He creates fun and tasty food to inspire everyone to eat healthier.

- Use Chef Jack's pictures to inspire you to create your own tasty food art.
- Make a sketch of the piece and, if possible, make it and take a picture of it.

Signs

Maggie is studying at Greenbow Primary School. She is very creative and has volunteered to help make signs. She created different symbols to put on the signs.

- Look at the signs Maggie made. Think of other signs that would be helpful at a Carnival celebration. Make sketches of the signs and then paint them.

Each of the people featured in the Ideas Express articles forms part of the population. How would we classify each one? Answer in your notebook.

Carnival

Carnival is celebrated before Lent begins (on Ash Wednesday). Carnival is a huge celebration full of fun, happiness and parties. People often go to fancy dress parties and wear fun and colourful masks.

Make your own Carnival mask!

1

Draw your mask on a piece of cardboard. Make holes for the eyes and elastic band.

2

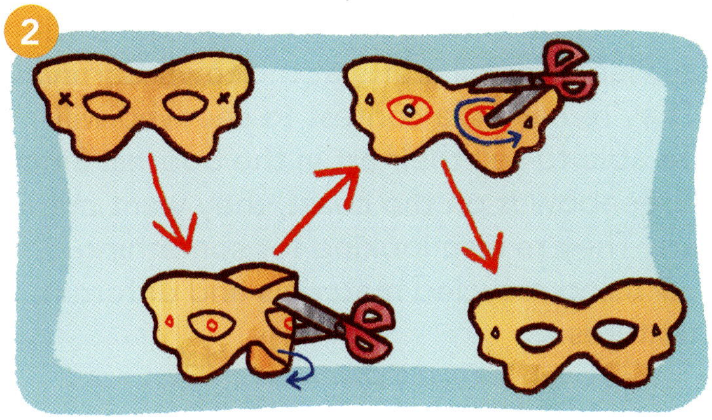

Cut out the holes by slighty bending the cardboard.

3

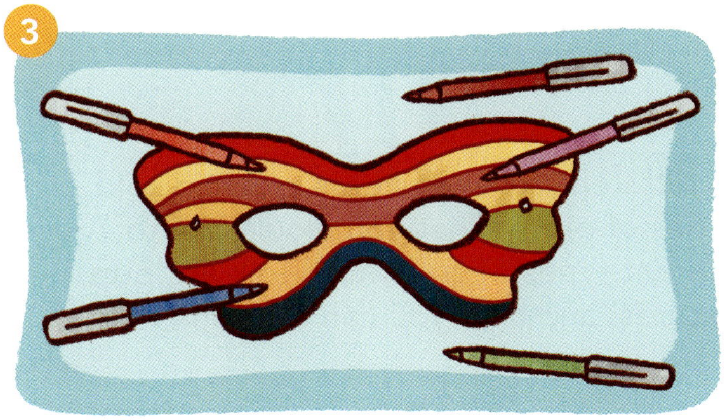

Colour your mask with felt-tip pens or tempera paints.

4

Glue on materials like sponge, caps, aluminium foil, paper or any other materials you would like.

5

Carefully insert the elastic band into the holes and tie a knot.

6

Enjoy your Carnival mask, by wearing it to a party!

IDEAS Carnival booth

INVESTIGATE

1. Have you ever been to a festival in your town? What types of things were sold there? Was food sold there? Were objects sold there?

DISCOVER

The city of Greenbow has two booths still available to sell crafts at the town Carnival. They're having a contest to see who will be able to sell their art in the booths. Since Greenbow is on the coast, they want marine art. They're also looking for something 3D using recycled materials and different textures.

2. What is craftwork? Do you often find craftwork in big department stores or at small fairs and Carnivals?

EXPLORE

3. Get into pairs or small groups. Think about different types of items you find sold in booths at fairs or Carnivals. Create sketches of pieces that you would like to create to sell at a Carnival. Think about different types of craftwork, folk art, pop art, the materials you can use (and their textures) and how you can combine this into a marine art piece.

APPLY

4. Use your sketch to help you create one of your pieces that you will sell in the booth at the Greenbow Carnival.

SUMMARY

5. As a class, display all of your pieces and talk about what inspired you, the materials you used and why you think it's the best piece to be sold at the Carnival.

6. Vote on which two are the winners of the contest and will be sold at the Greenbow Carnival.

Term 3

Surrealism

Surrealist paintings

Surrealism is a movement characterised by representing reality using fantasy, dreams and magic. The images can be real or unreal, but they are combined in a way that produces a dreamlike effect.

Galatea of the Spheres by Salvador Dalí (1952)

Salvador Dalí (1904 - 1989) and Joan Miró (1893 - 1983) were two very well-known Spanish painters. They were considered icons for the Surrealism movement in the 1920s. René Magritte (1898 - 1967) was another well-known Belgian Surrealist painter.

Create your own Surrealist painting

Dalí's painting *Galatea of the Spheres* is a Surrealist portrait of his wife, Gala. The features of her face are made up of floating spherical shapes. It was Dalís way of relating human existence with the universe.

Look at Magritte's paintings below. Why do you think the man's face and part of his body are made of a cage and two birds? Why is there a steam train coming out of the fireplace? Discuss the paintings with a partner. Interpret, or think about what the artist wanted to say.

The therapist by Magritte (1937)

Time transfixed by Magritte (1938)

- Think about an object, figure or landscape and change one of its elements to make it surprising and surreal. Use a piece of paper to draw or paint your scene. Show your classmates and take turns interpreting each others work.

Geometric drawings

Types of angles

An **angle** is formed when two straight lines meet. Angles are measured in degrees and there are three types of angles.

Right angles measure 90 degrees (90°).

Acute angles measure less than 90 degrees.

Obtuse angles measure more than 90 degrees.

Right angle

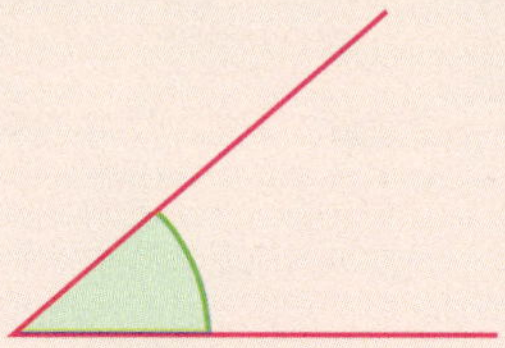
Acute angle

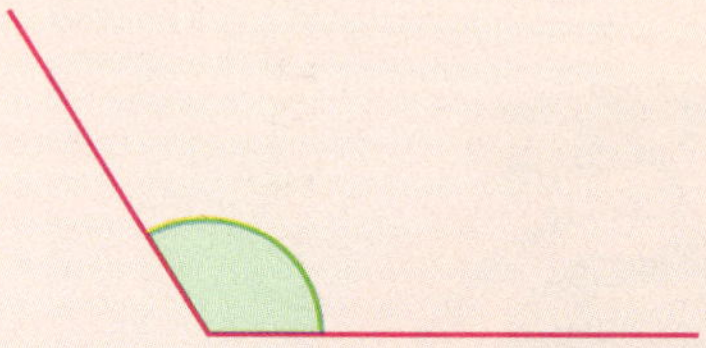
Obtuse angle

We measure angles with **protractors**. We can draw angles by using a protractor and a ruler.

Open fan

Pennants

Sandwich wedges

Caution sign

- Look at the objects. What types of angles are they?

Make your own protractor!

Use some cardboard and a compass to draw two identical circles. Then, use a ruler to draw a line through the middle of both. Lastly, draw a smaller circle inside each one.

Measure and mark different triangular shapes on only one of the circles.

Colour half of the other circle one solid colour. Colour the angles on the other circle with different colours.

Cut out the coloured ends of both circles. Be sure to include the entire, smaller circle on each one.

Attach both of the pieces to each other by aligning the smaller circles together. Make a small hole in the centre and put a brass fastener in it.

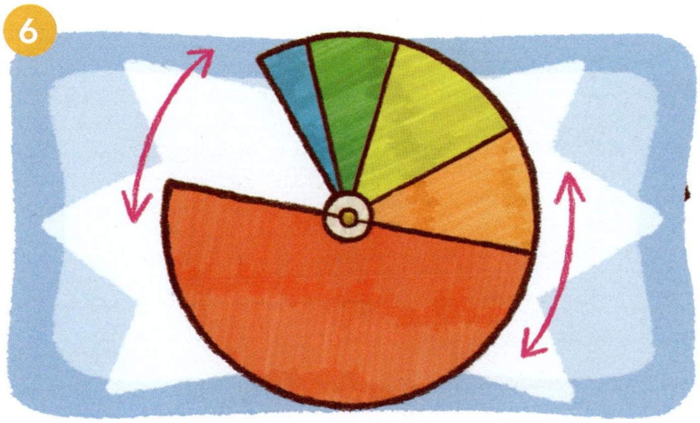

Congratulations, you've just made a working protractor!

Painting techniques

Chinese ink

Chinese ink is primarily used for Chinese and Japanese **calligraphy**, or writing. It is also used in traditional Chinese ink paintings. Chinese ink comes in many colours but the one mainly used for paintings is black. Black ink against white paper or silk creates a high contrast, monochrome painting. In order to achieve this contrast, the ink should not be diluted or mixed with water. Use a paintbrush or a quill. If you don't have a quill, you can sharpen a point on a piece of macaroni and use that!

Japanese writing

Traditional Chinese painting of a high mountain landscape

Paraffin wax and Chinese ink painting

Chinese ink can be used in other artistic techniques, like combining it with paraffin wax. Chinese ink is water soluble, so it can be mixed with more or less water to achieve different, lighter tones. Paraffin wax is oil-based and so it needs to be used first because the Chinese ink will slide off it and fill in the spaces that are wax-free.

- Follow the steps to use this technique on your painting.

Use white or light coloured cardboard.

Rub a candle along the paper in different shapes, lines and squiggles.

Apply the Chinese ink over the paper. You will see that the ink slides off and the wax drawing appears.

Now, repeat the steps, but this time, use the candle to draw a figure and watch it magically appear!

Still images and moving pictures

A **still image** is what we see in a picture, drawing or advertisement.

A **moving picture** is what we see in the cinema, on television or in a video. Moving pictures started with the invention of cinema in 1895.

Frame from *Avatar* (2009)

Cinema is a technique that consists of showing still images, or frames, so quickly that they look like they are moving. Television uses the same technique!

Video is the system used to record these images. It is easy and inexpensive to make our own videos nowadays with video cameras, mobiles phones or tablets.

Representing movement

In art, there are many things, like people, objects and plants, that give the sense of movement.

Movement can be represented in many forms of art, like drawings, painting and sculpture. This is done using different artistic techniques.

One of the techniques you can use is **blur**. You can blur in two ways: by gradually fading the intensity of the colour from more to less or from less to more.

Blurring or fading, can be done with your fingers, a paintbrush or with cotton wool.

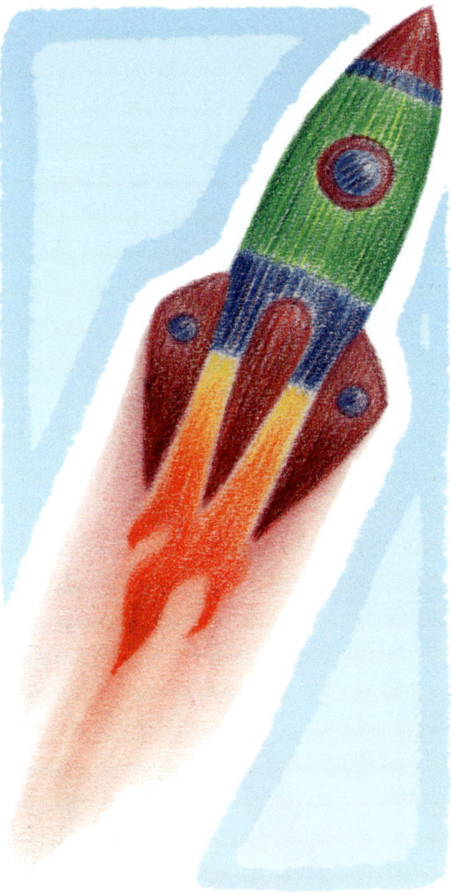

Coloured pencils

Lead pencil

Wax crayons

- Because of the blurring technique, the rocket in the drawings looks like it has been launched into space! Use a piece of paper and coloured pencils, wax crayons or a lead pencil to copy the rocket or draw anything you like. Blur it to create a sense of movement!

Technical drawings

Basic materials

Technical drawings are used to build houses, make cars, design mechanical parts and anything else that requires exact measurements. To draw them, you need the right tools like a compass, ruler, lead pencil, rubber and pencil sharpener.

A **compass** has got two parts. One holds the lead pencil in place and the other is a needle that helps you draw perfect circles and semicircles, or part of a circle!

A **scale ruler** is used for measuring and drawing straight lines.

There are two types of pencils: soft lead and hard lead. Hard lead pencils are darker and thinner and good for showing details. Soft lead pencils are lighter and thicker, so they are good for shading or blurring.

- Look at the objects below. Can you name them?

Tools used to make technical drawings.

Using a compass to draw

A compass is useful for drawing circles and semicircles. Look at the four drawings below and choose two that you would like to make a copy of.

Use your notebook and a compass to draw the circles or semicircles in the drawing.

If you choose to draw a semicircle, remember to hold the needle steady as if you were going to draw a full circle. Colour your drawings with coloured pencils or wax crayons.

Use a compass to draw the scoops of ice-cream and the dessert bowl.

Use a compass to draw the curved shape of the moon.

Use a compass to draw the street lamps.

Use a compass to draw the four circles of the target.

Painting classes

Paints and paintbrushes

Paintbrushes are used in art to draw and paint colours. Oil paints and watercolours are the two types of paint that are used most often.

Oil paints are made of pigments mixed with oils. They are usually blended with solvents like white spirit or turpentine so that the consistency is thicker or more fluid. Oil paint can be used on canvas, fabric, wood and other materials.

Artist working on an oil painting

Painting with tempera paints

Watercolours or tempera paints are diluted in water and can be used on paper or cardboard. Depending on how much water you mix the paint with, the colours can be light or almost transparent. Watercolour paints are thin and have the opposite effect as thick oil paints.

Using a paintbrush

Paintbrushes come in different sizes, from very thin, to very thick and wide. We can use a thin paintbrush to draw a line so thin that it looks like it was done with a hard, lead pencil!

We can use a thicker paintbrush to create a patch of colour like we can with wax crayons. No matter how thick or thin, we should always use soft strokes in only one direction and never rub the paintbrush on the surface.

Patches of colour

Lines

A bonfire has patches and lines

Patches of colour with lines

- Look at the examples above of the different techniques we can create when we use a paintbrush.

Egyptian architecture

The pyramids

The Egyptian **pyramids** are important monuments from Ancient History. The Great Pyramid of Giza, built for Cheops, is one of the Seven Wonders of the Ancient World. The Egyptians were experts at mathematical calculations and they had great organisational skills. These skills helped them build the pyramids using very simple methods. These methods included cutting stones with copper tools and pulling them up wooden ramps.

Great pyramid of Giza in Cairo, Egypt

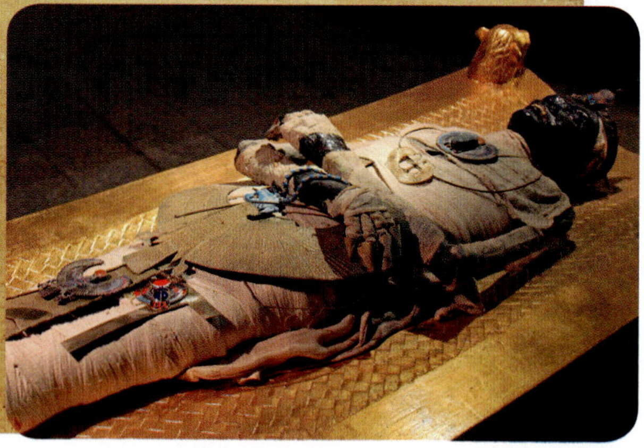

Ancient mummy

The pyramids were royal tombs for the pharaohs. Pharaohs were mummified and buried with all their belongings, amulets and even food and coins! The Egyptians believed that these things were necessary so that the body would reach Osiris. Osiris was the god of the afterlife.

Draw your own pyramids!

Use a light-coloured piece of cardboard and a ruler and follow the steps below.

1a

Draw the lines using a ruler.

1b

Use coloured pencils to first add the light tones and then the dark tones.

A mummy's sarcophagus

The **sarcophagus** was where the mummified body was placed. It was shaped like a human body and painted to look like a person. Pharaohs and important people were buried in a sarcophagus that was painted and richly decorated.

- Follow the steps to draw a mummy's sarcophagus

2a

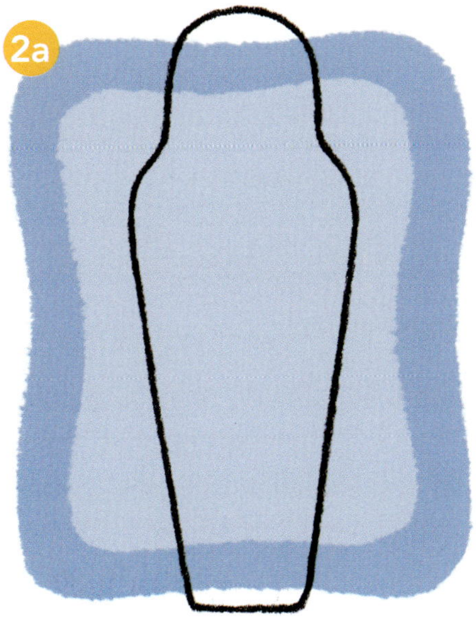

Draw the outline of the sarcophagus.

2b

Draw the rest of the lines.

2c

Add the details, colouring and decorating it however you would like!

Theatre: A snack at the Three Little Pigs' house

You are going to perform a play with your classmates. The main characters are:

Witch

Wolf

Three Little Pigs

Seven Dwarfs

Cinderella

Little Red Riding Hood

Snow White

Grandmother

 — Knock, knock.

 — Come in!

 — What an afternoon. With this rain, nobody can use a broom.

 — Hey! Don't close the door, I'm here!

 — Why be afraid of the wolf? Our house is made of brick. Hurray!

 — What's wrong? Are you joking? I just want a snack.

 — Me too, a delicious dish. I brought dessert from home.

 — Hey, a homemade dessert... from the chocolate house!

— Exactly! A couple of chocolate roof tiles with almonds.

— Chocolate with almonds? We really want a snack after working non-stop in the mine.

— Hello, hello.

— Here is the basket. Didn't Cinderella come?

— Here I am, with Snow White. My sisters can't come today. Oh, I brought you biscuits from my husband. Look, they have his name.

— She's right! Prince cookies.

— Well, look what I brought. Little Red Riding Hood, open the basket.

— Mmmm… It smells so good!

— It's a delicious pecan pie!

— I brought honey-salted peanuts and walnuts!

— Aahhhh! Oh no, we are allergic to nuts! We're sorry, but we can't snack on any of this!

— Oh no, what are we going to do?

— Grandmother, we are so absent-minded! We forgot that the three little pigs are allergic to nuts!

— Oh, what was I thinking? Why didn't I think?
I'm so sorry! Forgive me, little pigs!

— Don't worry grandmother! We all forgot, anybody can make a mistake.

— She's right. We all make mistakes.

— This can easily be solved.

— We can make a pie with mushrooms from our garden.

— That's true, we can all work together to pick the mushrooms. We have got to eat vegetables.

— Thank you, Wolf, and everyone else too, for understanding our feelings.

— Let's all go and pick mushrooms.

— And peppers and tomatoes.

— And asparagus and peas.

— Go while I prepare the fire.

— And I'll set the table, that's something I haven't done in a while.

— Well, Wolf, this time, when we return, don't come in through the chimney. Ha, ha, ha.

— Don't worry! I'll never do that again, because last time I burnt my…I burnt…ahem!

— Ha, ha, ha…how funny! That story was worth it.

— While we have our snack we can share lots of other stories.

— That's why we are here and we get together now and then!

deasexpress

Timelines

When we study the past, we often see different timelines. Some timelines are very simple line drawings with information. Others are more elaborate.

- Make a decorative timeline to represent the historical ages. Unscramble the words below. Create a timeline and illustrate it with important things that happened in each period of time.

lithicaeoalP

cihtiloeN

ernMod

ddMile

rarypotemCon

MACHINES AND ART

a

b

c

d

e
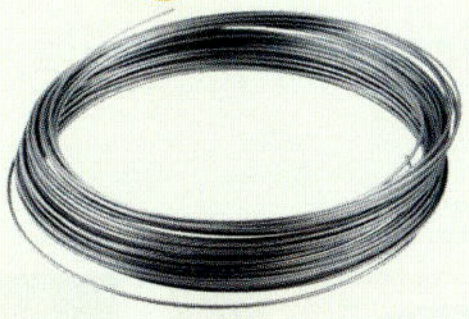

Machines come in all shapes and sizes, some are simple machines with no or few moving parts. Others are compound machines that are electric, electronic or mechanical. Artists and sculptors are sometimes inspired by these machines or their parts. In your notebook, name the parts and machines in the pictures.

- Create a sketch of how you could use these items in a sculpture.

ART AND THE METAL AGES

Throughout time, humans have continuously discovered new materials and ways of using them. During the Metal Ages humans discovered copper, bronze and iron. These materials are often used in sculpture by artists. Can you solve these riddles to figure out what the statues are made of?

- I was discovered around 6 500 years ago. I'm one of the first metals that humans worked with!
- I'm a mix of copper and tin. I'm a stronger metal and I've been used to make art as well as utensils.
- I can be found on the periodic table! I'm also one of the most common elements on Earth.

a

b

c
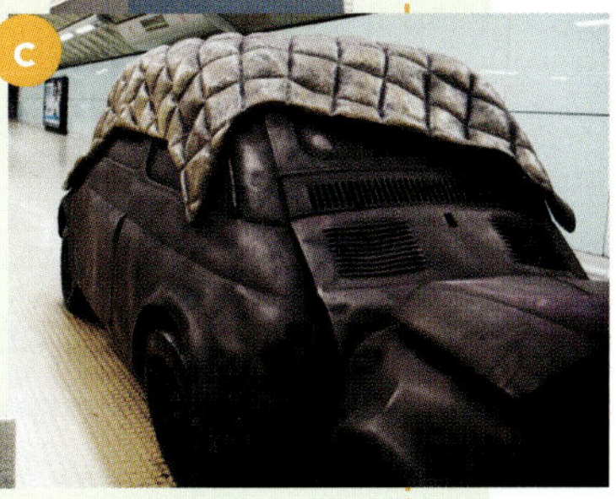

IDEAS Egyptian exhibition

INVESTIGATE

1. What do you know about Surrealism? What do you know about Egypt and mummies?

DISCOVER

The Brilliant Ideas Museum of Art is about to have an exhibition featuring mummies and Egypt. The directors of the museum want to create a comic strip about Egypt and mummies to advertise the show. They also want it done using Surrealism.

EXPLORE

2. Create a story board for your comic strip before getting started. You can make it a funny comic, a scary one, a historical one, use your imagination!
3. Create sketches of your pictures on a piece of paper. Be sure to keep the Surrealism style in mind when creating your sketch.

APPLY

4. Draw your comic and colour it in using coloured pencils, felt-tip pens or paints.

SUMMARY

5. Read your comic to the rest of the class and display it on the wall for everyone to see!